ESSAYS IN INTERNATIONAL ECONOMICS

No. 221, December 2000

—

LIFE AT THE TOP: INTERNATIONAL CURRENCIES IN THE TWENTY-FIRST CENTURY

—

BENJAMIN J. COHEN

INTERNATIONAL ECONOMICS SECTION

DEPARTMENT OF ECONOMICS
PRINCETON UNIVERSITY
PRINCETON, NEW JERSEY

INTERNATIONAL ECONOMICS SECTION
EDITORIAL STAFF

Library of Congress Cataloging-in-Publication Data

Cohen, Benjamin J.
    Life at the top: international currencies in the twenty-first century / Benjamin J. Cohen.
    p. cm. — (Essays in international economics; no. 221)
    Includes bibliographical references.
    ISBN 0-88165-128-1
    1. Dollar, American. 2. Euro 3. Yen, Japanese. 4. International finance I. Title.
II. Series.

HG540.C638 2000
332.4′5—dc21   00-065033
                                              CIP

Printed in the United States of America by Princeton University Printing Services at Princeton, New Jersey

International Standard Serial Number: 0071-142X
International Standard Book Number: 0-88165-128-1
Library of Congress Catalog Card Number: 00-065033

International Economics Section   Tel: 609-258-4048
  Department of Economics, Fisher Hall   Fax: 609-258-1374
  Princeton University   E-mail: ies@princeton.edu
  Princeton, New Jersey 08544-1021   Url: www.princeton.edu/~ies

CONTENTS

LIFE AT THE TOP: INTERNATIONAL CURRENCIES IN THE TWENTY-FIRST CENTURY

One of the most remarkable developments in global monetary relations at century's end is the rapid acceleration of cross-border competition among currencies—a spreading, market-driven phenomenon that I have elsewhere called the *deterritorialization* of money (Cohen, 1998). Circulation of national currencies is no longer confined within the territorial frontiers of nation-states. A few popular currencies, most notably the U.S. dollar and German deutsche mark (now being succeeded by the euro), have come to be widely used outside their country of origin, vying directly with local rivals for both medium-of-exchange and investment purposes. Competition is intense, and as in most competitions, success is largely a matter of survival of the fittest.

The result of this phenomenon has been a fundamental transformation of the *geography* of money, the broad configuration of global currency space. Where once existed a familiar landscape of relatively insular national monetary systems—in effect, a simple map of neatly divided territorial currencies—monies have now become both more entangled and more hierarchical. My image for this new geography is the Currency Pyramid: narrow at the peak, where the strongest currencies dominate, and increasingly broad below, reflecting varying degrees of competitive inferiority. A few monies enjoy the power and prestige of high rank; more constrained policy options are available to the issuers of many others. The highest standing is enjoyed by the dollar, the use of which predominates for most, if not all, cross-border purposes. Closest competition comes currently from the euro—newly created by Europe's Economic and Monetary Union (EMU)—and the Japanese yen, although neither currency can as yet claim anything like the universal appeal of America's greenback.

What are the prospects for today's top international currencies in the twenty-first century? The purpose of this essay is to take an objective new look at this critical question, giving particular emphasis to the factors most likely to influence the rivalry and rank of the top currencies over time. To put the discussion in perspective, I begin with a few basic statistics on cross-border currency use. I then explore the way in which the future of the top currencies may be influenced by the logic of market competition, the strategic preferences of national governments,

1

and prospective technological developments. Analysis suggests little near-term threat to the predominance of today's top currencies, although relative standing could be substantially altered by market competition, which in turn could lead to intensified policy competition among issuing authorities. Over the longer term, however, stretching further into the next century, technological developments could lead to the creation of entirely new rivals to today's top currencies, thereby transforming the geography of money virtually beyond recognition.

1 International Currencies

Currencies may be employed outside their country of origin for either of two purposes: for transactions between nations or for transactions within foreign states. The former purpose is conventionally referred to as "international" currency use, or currency "internationalization"; the latter is described as "currency substitution" and can be referred to as "foreign-domestic use." The top international monies are widely used for both purposes.

Both currency internationalization and currency substitution are products of intense market rivalry—a kind of Darwinian process of natural selection, driven by the force of demand, in which some monies such as the dollar, deutsche mark, and yen come to prevail over others for various commercial or financial purposes. Although cross-border use is known to be accelerating rapidly, its full dimensions cannot be measured precisely in the absence of comprehensive statistics on global currency circulation. Partial indicators, however, may be gleaned from a variety of sources to underscore the impressive orders of magnitude involved.

The clearest signal of the rapid growth of currency internationalization is sent by the global foreign-exchange market, where, according to the Bank for International Settlements (1999), average daily turnover has accelerated from $590 billion in 1989 (the first year for which such data are available) to $1.5 trillion in 1998—a rate of increase in excess of 25 percent per annum. Even allowing for the fact that much of this activity is accounted for by interdealer trading, the pace of expansion is impressive. The dollar is the most-favored vehicle for currency exchange worldwide, appearing on one side or the other of some 87 percent of all transactions in 1998 (little changed from its 90 percent share in 1989); the deutsche mark appeared in 30 percent of transactions and the yen in 21 percent. The dollar is also the most-favored vehicle for the invoicing of international trade, where it has been estimated to account

2

for nearly half of all world exports (Hartmann, 1998)—more than double America's actual share of world exports. The deutsche mark share of invoicing in recent years was 15 percent (roughly equal to Germany's proportion of world exports); the yen's share was 5 percent (significantly less than Japan's proportion of world exports).

A parallel story is evident in international markets for financial claims, including bank deposits and loans as well as bonds and stocks, all of which have grown at double-digit rates for years. Using data from a variety of sources, Thygesen et al. (1995) calculated what they call "global financial wealth," the world's total portfolio of private international investments. From just over $1 trillion in 1981, aggregate cross-border holdings quadrupled to more than $4.5 trillion by 1993—an expansion far greater than that of world output or trade in goods and services. Again, the dollar dominated, accounting for nearly 60 percent of foreign-currency deposits and close to 40 percent of international bonds. The deutsche mark accounted for 14 percent of deposits and 10 percent of bonds; the yen, for 4 percent of deposits and 14 percent of bonds. More recently, the International Monetary Fund ([IMF] 1999) put the total of international portfolio investments (including equities, long- and short-term debt securities, and financial derivatives) at just over $6 trillion in 1997.

The clearest signal of the rapid growth of currency substitution is sent by the rapid increase in the physical circulation of these same currencies outside their country of origin. For the dollar, an authoritative Federal Reserve study (Porter and Judson, 1996) puts the value of U.S. bank notes in circulation abroad in 1995 at between 55 and 70 percent of the total outstanding stock—equivalent to perhaps $250 billion in all. The same study also reckons that as much as three-quarters of the annual increase of U.S. notes now goes directly abroad, up from less than one-half in the 1980s and under one-third in the 1970s. Appetite for the dollar appears to be not only strong but growing. Using a comparable approach, Germany's Deutsche Bundesbank (1995) has estimated deutsche mark circulation outside Germany, mainly in East-Central Europe and the Balkans, at about 30 to 40 percent of total stock at end-1994, equivalent to some 65 billion to 90 billion deutsche marks ($45 billion to $65 billion). The deutsche mark's successor, the euro, is confidently expected to take over the deutsche mark's role in foreign-domestic use, once euro notes enter circulation in 2002, and perhaps even to cut into the dollar's market share. Similarly, on the other side of the world, Bank of Japan officials have been privately reported to believe that of the total supply of yen bank notes, amounting to some $370 billion in 1993, as much as 10 percent was located in neighboring countries (Hale, 1995). Combining these diverse estimates suggests a minimum total foreign circulation of the top currencies in the mid-1990s of at least $300 billion—by no means an inconsiderable sum and, judging from available evidence, apparently continuing to rise rapidly.

The evidence also suggests that a very wide range of countries is affected by this phenomenon, even if the precise numbers involved remain somewhat obscure. According to one authoritative source (Krueger and Ha, 1996), foreign bank notes accounted for 20 percent or more of the local money stock during the mid-1990s in as many as three dozen nations inhabited by at least one-third of the world's population. The same source also suggests that, in total, as much as 25 to 33 percent of the world's circulating currency was recently located outside its country of issue.

These numbers clearly confirm the growing importance of both international and foreign-domestic use of the top international currencies for both medium-of-exchange and store-of-value purposes. Most prominent, obviously, is the dollar, which remains by far the world's most popular choice for both currency internationalization and currency substitution. In effect, the dollar's domain spans the globe, from the Western Hemisphere to the former Soviet bloc and much of the Middle East; in all these regions, dollars circulate widely as a de facto parallel currency. Next is the deutsche mark, now being replaced by the euro, which is preeminent in monetary relations in much of the European neighborhood. In third place is the yen, albeit at some distance behind the first two. At the peak of the Currency Pyramid today, these three monies—the Big Three—plainly dominate.

2 Market Competition

But what of tomorrow? Will the Big Three continue to dominate, or can significant changes be expected? Broadly speaking, life at the top will be influenced most by three key considerations: the logic of market competition, the strategic preferences of national governments, and prospective technological developments. All three factors suggest that substantial new transformations in the geography of money are in the making.

Consider, first, the logic of market competition. Today's Big Three dominate, first and foremost, because they are (or have been) attractive to market participants for a variety of monetary purposes. If we

4

learn anything from the history of money, however, it is that monetary attractiveness can change—and with it, the relative standing of individual currencies. The past is littered with the carcasses of currencies that once dominated international commerce, from the Athenian drachma and Byzantine solidus (the bezant) to Florence's florin, Spain's (later Mexico's) silver peso, and, most recently, Britain's pound sterling. Shakespeare's words are as apt for money as they are for monarchs: "Uneasy lies the head that wears the crown." What does the logic of market competition tell us about who is likely to wear the crown tomorrow?

Attributes of Success

What makes a money attractive in the first place? The principal attributes required for competitive success in the international marketplace are familiar to specialists and are uncontroversial. Three features stand out.

The first requirement, at least during the initial stages of a currency's cross-border use, is widespread confidence in a money's future value backed by political stability in the country of origin. Essentially, this means a proven track record of relatively low inflation and inflation variability. High and fluctuating inflation rates increase the cost of acquiring information and performing price calculations. No currency is apt to be willingly adopted for international or foreign-domestic use if its purchasing power cannot be forecast with some degree of assurance.

Second are two qualities that I have elsewhere referred to as "exchange convenience" and "capital certainty" (Cohen, 1971), a high degree of transactional liquidity and reasonable predictability of asset value. The key to both is a set of well-developed financial markets, sufficiently open so as to ensure full access by nonresidents. Markets must not be encumbered by high transactions costs or formal or informal barriers to entry. They must also be broad, with a large assortment of instruments available for temporary or longer-term investment, and they must be deep and resilient, with fully operating secondary markets for most, if not all, financial claims.

Finally, and most important of all, a money must promise a broad transactional network, because nothing enhances a currency's acceptability more than the prospect of acceptability by others. Historically, this has usually meant an economy that is large in absolute size and well integrated into world markets. A large economy creates a naturally ample constituency for a currency; economies of scale are further enhanced if the issuing country is also a major player in world trade. No

5

money has ever risen to a position of international preeminence that was not initially backed by a leading economy. The greater the volume of transactions conducted in or with a given country, the greater are the potential network externalities to be derived from use of its money.

Reiteration of these essential attributes permits two broad inferences. First, among currencies in circulation today, there seems to be no candidate with even the remotest chance in the foreseeable future of challenging the top rank currently enjoyed by the dollar, euro, and yen. Second, among the Big Three, there seems a very real chance of significant shifts in relative market standing.

No New Challengers

The first inference follows logically from observable fact. We know that there is a great deal of inertia in currency use that can slow the transition from one equilibrium to another. Recall, for instance, how long it took the dollar to supplant the pound sterling at the top of the Currency Pyramid even after America's emergence a century ago as the world's richest economy. As Paul Krugman (1992, p. 173) has commented: "The impressive fact here is surely the inertia; sterling remained the first-ranked currency for half a century after Britain had ceased to be the first-ranked economic power." Similar inertias have been evident for millennia, as in the prolonged use of such international moneys as the bezant and silver peso long after the decline of the imperial powers that first coined them. It has also been evident more recently in the continued popularity of the dollar despite periodic bouts of exchange-rate depreciation. Such inertia seems very much the rule, not the exception, in currency relations.

Inertia is promoted by two factors. The first is the preexistence of an already well-established transactional network, which confers a natural advantage of incumbency. Once a particular money is widely adopted, not even a substantial erosion of its initial attractions—stable value, exchange convenience, or capital certainty—may suffice to discourage continued use. That is because switching from one currency to another necessarily involves an expensive process of financial adaptation. Considerable effort must be invested in creating and learning to use new instruments and institutions, with much riding on what other market agents may be expected to do at the same time. As attractive as some new contender may seem, adoption will not prove cost effective unless other agents appear likely to make extensive use of it too. The point is well put by Kevin Dowd and David Greenaway (1993, p. 1180): "Changing currencies is costly—we must learn to reckon in the new

6

currency, we must change the units in which we quote prices, we might have to change our records, and so on. . . . [This] explains why agents are often reluctant to switch currencies, even when the currency they are using appears to be manifestly inferior to some other."

The second factor is the exceptionally high level of uncertainty that is inherent in any choice among alternative moneys. The appeal of any money, ultimately, rests on an intersubjective faith in its general acceptability—something about which one can never truly be sure. Uncertainty thus encourages a tendency toward what psychologists call "mimesis": the rational impulse of risk-averse actors, in conditions of contingency, to minimize anxiety by imitative behavior based on past experience. Once a currency gains a degree of acceptance, its use is apt to be perpetuated—even after the appearance of powerful new challengers—simply by regular repetition of previous practice. In effect, a conservative bias is inherent in the dynamics of the marketplace. As one source has argued, "imitation leads to the emergence of a convention [wherein] emphasis is placed on a certain 'conformism' or even hermeticism in financial circles" (Orléan, 1989. pp. 81–83).

Because of this conservative bias, no new challenger can ever hope to rise toward the top of the Currency Pyramid unless it can first offer a substantial margin of advantage over existing incumbents. The dollar was able to do that in relation to sterling, once New York overtook London as the world's preeminent source of investment capital— although even that displacement, as Krugman notes, took a half century or more. Today, it is difficult to find any money anywhere with a comparable promise of competitive advantage with respect to the present Big Three.

Some sources suggest a possible future role for China's yuan, given the enormous size of the Chinese economy (already, by some measures, the second largest in the world) and its growing role in world trade. However broad the yuan's transactional network may eventually become, though, the currency's prospects suffer from the backwardness of China's financial markets and still lingering uncertainties about domestic political stability—to say nothing of the fact that use of the yuan continues to be inhibited by cumbersome exchange and capital controls. Similar deficiencies also rule out the monies of other large emerging markets, such as Brazil or India. Conversely, the still-independent currencies of some economically advanced countries, such as Switzerland or Canada, or even Britain, are precluded, despite obvious financial sophistication and political stability, by the relatively small size of the economies involved (Britain's pound, in any event, is expected

7

eventually to be absorbed into Europe's monetary union). Nowhere, in fact, does there seem to be any existing money with a reasonable chance of soon overcoming the powerful forces of inertia favoring today's incumbents. For the foreseeable future, the dominance of the Big Three seems secure.

Relative Shifts

Continued collective dominance, however, does not exclude the possibility of significant shifts in relative standing among the Big Three. At the top of the Currency Pyramid, the dollar today reigns supreme. But might that change? Could the dollar's market leadership be challenged any time soon by either the euro or the yen?

Less probability may be attached to a successful challenge by the yen than by the euro, despite Japan's evident strengths as the world's top creditor nation and its enviable record of success in controlling inflation and promoting exports. Cross-border use of the yen did accelerate significantly in the 1980s, during the glory years of Japanese economic expansion. Internationalization was particularly evident in bank lending and in securities markets, where yen-denominated claims were especially attractive to investors. But the yen never came close to overtaking the popularity of the dollar, or even the deutsche mark, and it was little used for either trade invoicing or currency substitution. Its upward trajectory, moreover, was abruptly halted in the 1990s, following the bursting of Japan's "bubble economy," and there seems little prospect of resumption in the near term so long as Japanese domestic stagnation persists. In fact, use of the yen abroad in recent years has, in relative terms, decreased rather than increased, mirroring Japan's economic troubles at home. These difficulties include not only a fragile banking system but also a level of public debt, relative to GDP, that is now the highest of any industrial nation. Japanese government bonds have already been downgraded by rating agencies, discouraging investors. The decline of foreign use of the yen has been most striking in neighboring Asian countries, where bank loans and other Japanese investments have been rolled back dramatically. "The country's financial muscle in Asia is waning," reports the *New York Times*, "Japanese investment in the region may never be the same" ("Japan's Light Dims in Southeast Asia," December 26, 1999, p. BU1).

The biggest problem for the international standing of the yen is Japan's financial system, which despite recent improvements, has long lagged behind American and even many European markets in terms of openness or efficiency. Indeed, as recently as two decades ago, Japanese

8

financial markets remained the most tightly regulated and protected in the industrial world, preventing wider use of the yen. Strict exchange controls were maintained on both inward and outward movements of capital; securities markets were relatively underdeveloped; and financial institutions were rigidly segmented. Starting in the mid-1970s, a process of liberalization began, prompted partly by a slowing of domestic economic growth and partly by external pressure from the United States. Exchange controls were largely eliminated; new instruments and markets were developed; and institutional segmentation was relaxed—all of which did much to enhance the yen's exchange convenience and capital certainty. Most dramatic was a multiyear liberalization program announced in 1996, dubbed the "Big Bang" in imitation of the swift deregulation of Britain's financial markets a decade earlier.

The reform process, however, is still far from complete and could take many years to come even close to approximating market standards in the United States or Europe. One recent study applauds the prospective shakeout of the Japanese banking sector but admits that the transition is unlikely to be fully executed for at least another decade (Hoshi and Kashyap, 2000). Other sources are even less encouraging, questioning whether Japan's public authorities have the political will needed to overcome determined resistance from powerful vested interests. Both Ito and Melvin (2000) and Schaede (2000) emphasize the extent to which success of the Big Bang will depend on completion of complementary reforms in tax codes, regulatory processes, and the institutions of law enforcement and legal recourse—initiatives that would require fundamental changes in the way business is done in Japan. Tokyo's politicians have so far shown little enthusiasm for such radical transformation. Yet, without further progress, the yen will remain at a competitive disadvantage relative to both the dollar and euro. International traders and investors will have little incentive to bear the costs and risks of switching from either of the other top currencies to the yen. Indeed, the trend is more likely to continue moving the other way, toward a gradual erosion of the yen's relative standing in a manner reminiscent of sterling's long decline in an earlier era.

More probability, by contrast, can be attached to a successful challenge by the euro, which started life in January 1999 with most of the key attributes necessary for competitive success already well in evidence. Together, the eleven current members of EMU—familiarly known as "Euroland"—constitute a market nearly as large as that of the United States, with extensive trade relations not only in the European region, but also around the world. The potential for network externalities is

9

considerable. Euroland also starts with both unquestioned political stability and an enviably low rate of inflation backed by a joint monetary authority, the European Central Bank (ECB), that is fully committed to preserving confidence in the euro's future value. Much room exists, therefore, for a quick ascendancy for the euro as an international currency, just as most observers predict (for example, Bergsten, 1997; Hartmann, 1998; Portes and Rey, 1998). The new currency has already begun to surpass the past aggregate share of the deutsche mark and other EMU currencies in foreign trade and investment. The only question is how high the euro will rise and how much business it will take from the dollar.

As with the yen, the answer rests first and foremost on prospective developments in financial markets. Even with the euro's promise of broad economies of scale and stable purchasing power, the dollar will be favored by the natural advantages of incumbency unless euro transactions costs, which historically have been higher than those on the more widely traded dollar, can be lowered to more competitive levels. The level of euro transactions costs will, in turn, depend directly on what happens to the structure of Europe's financial markets as the merger of Euroland currencies proceeds. Without sustained improvements in market efficiency and openness, it will be difficult for the euro to overcome the forces of inertia characteristic of international currency use. Richard Portes and Hélène Rey (1998, p. 308) put the point most succinctly: "The key determinant of the extent and speed of internationalization of the euro will be transaction costs in foreign exchange and securities markets."

In fact, prospects for the structural efficiency of Europe's financial system seem good. On a purely quantitative basis, introduction of the euro will eventually create the largest single-currency financial market in the world. The aggregate value of Euroland financial claims (bonds, equities, and bank loans) is already almost as large as that of the United States and will undoubtedly keep growing in the future. Beyond that, there are bound to be significant qualitative improvements in market depth and liquidity, as previously segmented national markets are gradually knitted together into one integrated whole. The elimination of exchange risk inside EMU has already intensified competition between financial institutions, particularly in such hotly contested activities as bond underwriting and syndicated bank lending, encouraging cost-cutting and innovation. Over the longer term, harmonization of laws and conventions and the development of new cross-border payments systems will enhance the marketability of assets of all kinds. Progress to date has

10

been swiftest in money markets and the corporate bond market, where instruments and procedures are already largely standardized. Primary equity markets have also expanded rapidly, along with efforts to merge national stock exchanges. Although a projected merger of the Frankfurt and London exchanges failed to materialize, a successful partnership has been created by the bourses of Paris, Amsterdam, and Brussels under the label "Euronext." Full consolidation of markets for government bonds, it is expected, will take longer, owing to the persistence of differential credit and liquidity risk premiums between countries.

There is little reason to doubt that these improvements will have a substantial effect on international investment practice. Curiously, foreign savers and portfolio managers have been slower than anticipated to add to their holdings of euro-denominated assets, as compared with investments in EMU currencies in the past, despite the greater depth and liquidity on offer. Most likely, the comparatively low demand has been due to uncertainties about the euro's exchange rate, which has declined throughout the currency's first two years in existence. But the impact of EMU is already clearly evident on the borrowing side, where nonresidents have been attracted by the opportunity to tap into a much broader pool of savings. In bond and money markets, new foreign issues jumped sharply after the euro's introduction. Indeed, in the second half of 1999, euro-denominated international bond and notes issuance actually exceeded dollar issuance for the first time. Equity issues also grew substantially, and the euro share of international bank lending rose by several percentage points. Comprehensive surveys of the euro's first year (Danthine, Giavazzi, and von Thadden, 2000; Detken and Hartmann, 2000) agree that major changes are occurring in the European financial landscape.

Yet, the question remains: Will Europe's structural improvements lower euro transactions costs enough to overcome the powerful conservative bias inherent in the dynamics of the marketplace? About that, legitimate doubts remain. Certainly, much of the increase of business in euros will come at the expense of the dollar, reducing the dollar's present margin of leadership. But it seems equally certain that anticipated efficiency gains in Europe's financial markets, although substantial, are unlikely on their own to suffice to displace the dollar from top rank. Neither Danthine, Giavazzi, and von Thadden (2000) nor Detken and Hartmann (2000) find much evidence of reduced transactions costs to date. In any event, no one expects that market spreads for the euro will ever decline to a level significantly below those currently quoted for the dollar. Spontaneous market developments will therefore almost surely

11

have to be reinforced by deliberate policy actions for the crown to pass securely to the euro. Again, Portes and Rey (1998, p. 310) put the point most succinctly: "If they wish to promote the emergence of the euro as an international currency, European authorities must make the domestic euro financial markets more efficient, more integrated and cheaper for participants."

In short, the logic of market competition tells us that in all likelihood, the only serious challenge to the dollar in coming years will be from the euro—not from the yen and, most certainly, not from any other existing national currency. Even for the euro, however, success will be determined not just by market developments, but also by official policy actions. This brings us to the subject of the strategic preferences of governments.

3 Government Preferences

No discussion of currency relations can ignore government preferences. States have long placed a high value on control of the issue and management of money—commonly referred to as "national monetary sovereignty." We know, of course, that in a number of countries, private monies exist, sometimes in fairly sizable numbers (L. Solomon, 1996). But we also know that all such monies remain deliberately local, circulating on a very restricted scale. The currencies that really matter in today's world are state currencies: the progeny of independent national governments (or several governments acting collectively in a monetary union). Currency outcomes, as a consequence, are inherently political, not just economic. The future of national currencies, including the Big Three, will depend not only on the logic of market competition but also on the nature of state behavior.

From Monopoly to Oligopoly

National policy choices were relatively simple when money was largely territorial. Currency domains could be assumed to coincide precisely with the political frontiers of states. Governments could legitimately aspire to exercise a monopoly control within their own jurisdiction over the issue and management of money.

It is easy to see why a monetary monopoly might be highly prized by governments. Genuine power resides in the command that money represents. A strictly territorial currency confers four main benefits: a potent political symbol to promote a sense of national identity; a potentially powerful source of revenue, seigniorage (otherwise known as

12

the "inflation tax"), to underwrite public expenditures; a possible instrument to manage the macroeconomic performance of the economy; and a practical means to insulate the nation from foreign influence or constraint. Absolute monetary sovereignty clearly privileges the interests of government in relation to societal actors—a privilege that, over time, has been wisely used by some and badly abused by many others.

A map of neatly divided territorial currencies is still the geography that most people think of, insofar as they think about currency space at all. It is also the geography that most people think has prevailed for all time, as if monetary relations could never be configured in any other way. In fact, nothing is further from the truth. Monetary geography is not written in stone, and territorial currencies are, in historical terms, of quite recent origin. Prior to the 1800s, no government even thought to claim a formal monopoly over the issue and use of money within its political domain. Cross-border circulation of currencies was not only accepted but widespread and commonplace. The notion of absolute monetary sovereignty began to emerge only in the nineteenth century, with the formal consolidation of the powers of nation-states in Europe and elsewhere, and reached its apogee only in the middle of the twentieth century. Since then, the tide has clearly reversed—all part of the broadening globalization of the world economy that has been going on since World War II. Driven by the pressures of competition and technological innovation, national financial and monetary systems have become increasingly integrated, effectively widening the array of currency choice for many transactors and investors. As a result, strictly territorial currencies are fast disappearing in most parts of the world. Today, as we enter the twenty-first century, money is becoming increasingly deterritorialized.

Currency deterritorialization poses a new and critical challenge to policymakers. No longer able to exert the same degree of control over the circulation of their monies, governments are driven to compete, inside and across borders, for the allegiance of market actors—in effect, to fight for market share, much as rival firms in an oligopolistic industry compete. Their targets are the users of money, at home or abroad. Their aim is to sustain or enhance a currency's appeal, almost as if monies were goods to be sold under registered trademarks. As Robert Aliber (1987, p. 153) has quipped, "the dollar and Coca-Cola are both brand names. . . . Each national central bank produces its own brand of money. . . . Each national money is a differentiated product. . . . Each central bank has a marketing strategy to strengthen the demand for its particular brand of money." Monopoly, in short, has yielded to something more like oligopoly, and monetary governance is rapidly being reduced to little more than a choice among marketing strategies designed to shape and manage demand. The management of money, at its most basic, has become a political contest for market loyalty.

Furthermore, all states must be considered part of the oligopolistic struggle, no matter how competitive or uncompetitive their respective currencies may be. Rivalry is not limited merely to the trio of monies at the peak of the Currency Pyramid, as is sometimes suggested (De Boissieu, 1988). That would be so only if cross-border competition were restricted to international use alone—if the Big Three currencies, along with a few minor rivals (for example, sterling and the Swiss franc), were vying for shares of private investment portfolios or for use in trade invoicing. Deterritorialization, however, extends to foreign-domestic use as well—to currency substitution as well as currency internationalization—thus involving all national currencies, in direct competition with one another to some degree, the weak as well as the strong. Money's oligopoly is truly global.

The question is, in this new oligopolistic setting driven by the logic of market competition, how can governments be expected to respond to emerging rivalries at the peak of the Currency Pyramid? Outcomes will be determined jointly by two sets of state actors—those at the peak of the pyramid (the United States, Euroland, and Japan) and those below. I shall examine each group in turn.

Leadership Rivalries

At the peak of the Currency Pyramid, anticipated shifts in relative standing among the Big Three currencies will almost certainly trigger enhanced policy competition across both the Atlantic and the Pacific. The reason is simple. Much is at stake, and the benefits of market leadership will not be conceded without a struggle.

Although minimized by some (for example, Wyplosz, 1999, pp. 97–100), the benefits of market leadership can be considerable. Most discussion focuses primarily on seigniorage: the implicit transfer, equivalent to a subsidized or interest-free loan, that goes to a country when its money is widely used and held abroad. Seigniorage income, on its own, is unlikely to be large enough to spark significant policy conflict. This fact, however, ignores two other material gains that, although less easily quantified, are apt to be considered much more important. One is the increased flexibility of macroeconomic policy that is afforded by the privilege of being able to rely on domestic currency to help finance external deficits. The other is the political power that

14

derives from the monetary dependence of others. Not only is the issuing country better insulated from outside influence or coercion in the domestic policy arena. It is also better positioned to pursue foreign objectives without constraint or even to exercise a degree of influence or coercion internationally. Political power may be employed bilaterally or, alternatively, through the mechanisms of a multilateral agency such as the IMF, where market leaders are bound to have disproportionate sway. As much was admitted to me once by a highly placed U.S. Treasury official, who confided that in Washington policy circles, the IMF was viewed as "a convenient conduit for U.S. influence" (Cohen, 1986, p. 229).

To this list, some would also add the international status and prestige that goes with market leadership. Widespread circulation of a currency is a constant reminder of the issuing country's elevated rank in the community of nations. Certainly, foreign publics cannot help but be impressed when another nation's money successfully penetrates the domestic financial system and gains widespread acceptance. "Great powers have great currencies," Robert Mundell (1996, p. 10) once wrote. Although policymakers may be loath to admit it, such reputational considerations are apt to be given some importance too.

Admittedly, there are limits to most of these benefits. All are likely to be greatest in the early stages of cross-border use, when confidence in a money is at a peak. Later on, as external liabilities accumulate, increasing supply relative to demand, gains may be eroded, particularly if there is an attractive alternative available. Foreigners may legitimately worry about the risk of future devaluation or even restrictions on the usability of their holdings. Thus, the market leader's policy behavior may eventually be constrained, to a degree, by a need to discourage sudden or substantial conversions through the exchange market. Both seigniorage income, on a net basis, and macroeconomic flexibility will be reduced if a sustained increase of interest rates is required to maintain market share. Similarly, overt exploitation of political power will be inhibited if foreigners can switch allegiance easily to another currency. Even admitting such limits, however, numerous sources acknowledge that these are advantages worth fighting for (see, for example, Portes and Rey, 1998, pp. 308–310). There is more than enough incentive here to motivate policymakers. Enhanced competition among the Big Three should therefore come as no surprise.

Consider Europe, for example, whose new monetary union creates a golden opportunity to bid for higher market standing. Officially, European aspirations remain modest. According to an authoritative statement

15

by the ECB (1999, p. 31), the development of the euro as an international currency—if it happens at all—will be mainly a market-driven process, simply one of many possible byproducts of EMU. Euro internationalization "is not a policy objective [and] will be neither fostered nor hindered by the Eurosystem. . . . The Eurosystem therefore adopts a neutral stance" (ECB, 1999, p. 45). But these carefully considered words may be dismissed as little more than diplomatic rhetoric, revealing nothing. Behind the scenes, it is known that there is considerable disagreement among policymakers, with the eventual direction of policy still unsettled. Many in Europe are indeed inclined to leave the future of the euro to the logic of market competition. But many others, aware of the strong incumbency advantages of the dollar, favor a more proactive stance to reinforce EMU's potential. EMU has long been viewed in some circles, particularly in France, as the European Union's best chance to challenge the long-resented hegemony of the dollar.

Much more revealing, therefore, is not what the ECB says, but what it does. Especially suggestive is the bank's controversial decision to plan issues of euro notes in denominations as high as 100, 200, and 500 euros—sums far greater than most Eurolanders are likely to find useful for everyday transactions when euro bills and coins begin to circulate in 2002. Why issue such notes? Informed sources suggest that the plan may have been decided in order to reassure the German public, fearful of losing their beloved deutsche mark, that notes comparable to existing high-denomination deutsche mark bills would be readily available. But that is hardly the whole story. As knowledgeable experts like Kenneth Rogoff (1998) and Charles Wyplosz (1999) observe, it is also likely that the decision had something to do with the familiar phenomenon of dollarization: the already widespread circulation of large-denomination dollar notes, especially $100 notes, in various parts of the world. Dollarization translates conservatively into an interest saving for the U.S. government, a form of seigniorage earnings, of at least $15 billion a year (Blinder, 1996)—not a huge profit, but nonetheless enough, apparently, to persuade EMU's authorities to plan on offering a potentially attractive alternative. As Rogoff (1998, p. 264) has written: "Given the apparently overwhelming preference of foreign and underground users for large-denomination bills, the [ECB's] decision to issue large notes constitutes an aggressive step toward grabbing a large share of developing country demand for safe foreign currencies."

How will Washington react? Officially, the U.S. remains unconcerned. "The emergence of the euro as an international currency should not be viewed with alarm," writes the President's Council of Economic Advisers

(1999, p. 297). "It is unlikely that the dollar will be replaced anytime soon" (p. 299). Policy statements regarding the prospective challenge of the euro have been studiously neutral, asserting that EMU is Europe's business, not America's. But these words, too, may be dismissed as diplomatic rhetoric, concealing as much as they reveal. As Portes (1999, p. 34) writes: "It is difficult to believe that the American authorities are indifferent." In fact, in Washington, as in Europe, there is still much disagreement behind the scenes about the eventual direction of policy, and especially in the Congress, there is much pressure to respond to the Europeans in kind. Already a proposal to offer a $500 note to rival the ECB's large-denomination bills has been circulated on Capitol Hill (Makinen, 1998, p. 5). Legislation has even been introduced to encourage developing countries to adopt the dollar formally as a replacement for their own national currencies—*official* dollarization, as the idea has come to be known. As an incentive, Washington would offer a specified share of the resulting increase in U.S. seigniorage earnings. Policy support for official dollarization is being actively promoted by the Joint Economic Committee of the Congress (1999).

More generally, given the considerable benefits of market leadership, there seems every reason to expect Euroland and the United States to compete vigorously to sustain or promote demand for their respective currencies. Many Europeans clearly wish to see the euro established on a par with the dollar as an international currency. What more can Europe do, apart from issuing high-denomination notes? International investments in euro bonds and stocks, which, as indicated, have lagged until now, might be encouraged with selected tax incentives, including abolition of any withholding or reporting requirements. Likewise, cross-border use of the euro as a vehicle currency might be underwritten with targeted subsidies for European banks, lowering the cost of commercial credit for third-country trade. In so doing, however, Euroland would also put itself on track for open confrontation with the United States. Aggressive policy initiatives from one side of the Atlantic will almost certainly provoke more retaliatory countermeasures from the other side, along lines already being mooted in Washington. Competition is likely to be intense and possibly nasty.

The same can be expected across the Pacific as well, where Japan has given every indication that it, too, intends to stay in the fray, actively battling to preserve as much as possible of the yen's currently fragile international role—in East Asia at least, if not beyond. One straw in the wind came in 1996, when Japan signed a series of agreements with nine neighboring countries to lend their central banks yen if needed to help

17

stabilize exchange rates. Informed sources had no doubt that these pacts were deliberately designed to increase Japanese influence among members of an eventual yen bloc. "It's a manifest attempt to take leadership," said one bank economist in Tokyo (*New York Times*, April 27, 1996, p. 20). And an even stronger indicator came in 1997, after the first shock waves of the Asian financial crisis, when Tokyo seized upon the occasion to propose a new regional financial facility—quickly called the Asian Monetary Fund (AMF)—to help protect local currencies against speculative attack. The AMF proposal was by far the most ambitious effort yet by Japan to implement a strategy of market leadership in Asian finance. Tokyo's initiative was successfully blocked by the United States, which publicly expressed concern about a possible threat to the central role of the IMF. Privately, it was clear that Treasury officials were even more concerned about a possible threat to the dominance of the dollar in the region. Nonetheless, the idea continues to attract favorable interest (Bergsten, 1998).

Moreover, despite economic troubles at home and the steady repatriation of private investments from abroad, Tokyo has persisted in seeking new ways to promote its monetary role in the region (Hughes, 2000). In October 1998, Finance Minister Kiichi Miyazawa offered some $30 billion in fresh financial aid for Asia in a plan soon labeled the "New Miyazawa Initiative." Two months later, he made it clear that Japan had every intention of reviving its AMF proposal when the time seemed right (*Financial Times*, December 16, 1998, p. 1). Similarly, in late 1999, Japanese authorities floated a plan to drop two zeros from the yen (which is currently valued at near one hundred yen for either the dollar or the euro) in order to facilitate its use in foreign transactions. Simplifying the currency's denomination, said one official, "might have a positive effect in that the yen would be more internationally easy to understand" (*New York Times*, November 19, 1999, p. C4). Commented a foreign banker in Tokyo: "If there's a liquid market in dollars and a liquid market in euros, there's a risk of Japan becoming a sort of second-string market. . . . They don't want the yen to become the Swiss franc of Asia" (*New York Times*, November 19, 1999, p. C4). Most recently, in May 2000, Tokyo engineered an agreement among thirteen regional governments on a new network of swap arrangements centered on the yen ("Asian Currencies," 2000, p. 76–77). Clearly, Tokyo does not intend to allow further erosion of its currency's standing without a fight.

But here too, as in Europe, aggressive policy initiatives will almost certainly put the Japanese on track for confrontation with the United States. Even a yen-bloc enthusiast like David Hale (1995, p. 162) acknowledges that "there is also a risk that [such measures] will be interpreted as a threat by some Americans [and] could intensify the economic conflicts that are already straining U.S.-Japan relations." Yen competition with the dollar is likely to be no less heated than the expected dollar-euro rivalry, and could be even nastier. Market leadership will continue to be the strategic preference of proponents for all the Big Three currencies.

Follower Options

But will other currencies follow? For countries lower down in the Currency Pyramid, fallout from intensified rivalry among the Big Three will be unavoidable. Governments across the globe will be compelled to reconsider their own strategic preferences. Outcomes, however, are likely to be far less uniform than many predict.

Most common is the prediction that growing currency deterritorialization and heightened competition for market leadership will encourage the emergence of two or three large monetary blocs centered on the dollar, euro, and, possibly, the yen (Eichengreen, 1994; Beddoes, 1999; Hausmann, 1999). Governments will seek to shelter themselves from possible currency turmoil by subordinating their monetary sovereignty to one of the top international currencies by way of a firm exchange-rate rule—in effect, a strategy of market "followership" (analogous to passive price followership in an oligopoly). Linkage could take the form of a tight single-currency peg or, more radically, could be implemented by means of an ostensibly irrevocable currency board or even official dollarization ("euroization?" "yenization?").

Market followership would naturally be attractive to countries that have particularly close economic or political ties to one of the dominant financial powers. These might include many of the states of Latin America, ever in the shadow of the United States, states from the former Soviet bloc, or states in the Mediterranean basin or Sub-Saharan Africa that have close ties to Europe. The dollar already serves as nominal anchor for a number of smaller countries in the Caribbean and Pacific, as well as in scattered locations elsewhere. The euro does the same for several currency boards in East-Central Europe as well as in the CFA Franc Zone, having seamlessly assumed the role in francophone Africa previously played by the French franc. Patrick Honohan and Philip Lane (1999) suggest that more African currencies will soon be tied to the euro. Other sources confidently predict that pegs to the euro will soon be adopted by many Mediterranean countries as well (Bénassy-Quéré and Lahrèche-Révil, 1999). The debate has also been

19

reopened in Latin America about closer ties to the dollar (Dornbusch, 1999; Hausmann et al., 1999; Levy Yeyati and Sturzenegger, 2000).

In the past, such ideas might have been dismissed as politically naive. All kinds of problems could be cited, from the loss of a lender of last resort under a currency board to the loss of seigniorage with dollarization. But that was before Argentina, which, despite a well-known history of the most intense nationalism, successfully opted for a dollar-based currency board in 1991—and whose former president, before leaving office late last year, even proposed replacing Argentina's peso altogether with the dollar. In the context of the coming rivalry among the Big Three, the Argentine case is now considered instructive. A strategy of irrevocable market followership no longer seems a fantasy. As Rudiger Dornbusch (1999, p. 8) puts the point, with characteristic flair: "The lesson is obvious: Europe's periphery should adopt the Euro on a currency board basis or fully. And in the same spirit, Latin America should follow the Argentine example of a currency board on the US dollar or outright dollarization." In January 2000, Ecuador became the first to follow Dornbusch's advice, announcing plans to replace its national currency with the dollar; several other Latin American governments were reported to be considering similar initiatives.

But what of countries that might prefer *not* to be dominated, whether by the United States or by Europe (or Japan)? Not all governments can be expected to acquiesce willingly in a passive strategy of market followership. Other options exist, from free floating to various contingent exchange-rate rules, such as a loose single-currency peg or basket peg, a crawling peg, or target zones of one kind or another. There is every reason to believe that governmental preferences are likely to be correspondingly diverse.

Opinions differ on whether the full range of these options is actually available in practice. According to some observers, neither free floating nor irrevocably fixed rates can be regarded as truly viable options. Fixed rates, we are told, are too rigid, creating the risk of prolonged misalignments and payments disequilibria, and flexible rates are too volatile and prone to speculative pressures. The only real choices are intermediate regimes that promise a degree of adaptability without generating undue uncertainty—"stable but adjustable rates," to borrow a phrase from an earlier era. "Quite the contrary," retort others, who insist that it is the intermediate choices that are discredited, not the extreme "corner solutions," owing to the great increase of international capital mobility in recent decades. This view is rapidly gaining popularity among specialists today. The middle ground of contingent rules has in effect been "hollowed out," as Barry Eichengreen (1994) memorably put it.

In reality, however, neither corner solutions nor contingent rules are discredited, for the simple reason that in an imperfect world, there is no perfect choice. All such views rest on implicit—and questionable— political judgments about what tradeoffs may or may not be tolerable to policymakers. Eichengreen's hollowing-out hypothesis, for example, clearly assumes that governments will be unwilling to pay the price of coping with occasional speculative crises. Defenders of contingent rules, conversely, assume that governments will naturally prefer to avoid absolute commitments of any kind—whether to an irrevocable exchange rate or to market determination of currency values—whatever the cost. The reality, as Jeffrey Frankel (1999) has persuasively argued, is that such tradeoffs are made all the time when exchange-rate regimes are decided. No option is ruled out *a priori*.

The political dimension of exchange-rate choice tends to be discounted in conventional economic models, where policymakers are assumed to be concerned more or less exclusively with maximizing output and minimizing inflation in the context of an open economy subject to potentially adverse shocks. In fact, political factors enter in two ways. First, the calculus is affected by domestic politics: the tug and pull of organized interest groups of every kind. The critical issue is the familiar one of whose ox is gored. Who wins and who loses? The material interests of specific constituencies are systematically influenced by what a government decides to do with its money. Policy design and implementation are bound to be sensitive to the interplay among domestic political forces.

Second, the utility function of policymakers includes more than just macroeconomic performance. As a practical matter, sovereign governments worry about other things, too—not least, about their own policy autonomy, their scope for discretion to pursue diverse objectives in the event of unforeseen developments, up to and including war. Key in this regard is the domestic seigniorage privilege—called by one source a state's "revenue of last resort" (Goodhart, 1995, p. 452). The more tightly a currency is pegged, the less room policymakers have to resort at will to inflationary money creation to augment public spending when deemed necessary. Monetary firmness is gained, but at a loss of fiscal flexibility. Certainly, it is not wrong to attach importance to a reduction of exchange-rate uncertainty, which can promote trade and investment and squeeze out risk premia in interest rates. But in an insecure world, governments may be forgiven for attaching importance to currency

21

flexibility, too, as a defense against *political* uncertainty. Policy design and implementation are bound to be sensitive to the interplay among such considerations as well.

For all these reasons, therefore, strategic preferences are apt to vary considerably, depending on the unique circumstances of each country. Although followership may be attractive to some, a more neutral stance will appeal to states with more diversified external relations, political as well as economic. Such states might include those in Japan's neighborhood in East Asia, which trade as much with the United States, and nearly as much with Europe, as they do with Japan, and which prefer to maintain equally cordial ties with all three centers of the industrial world. Indeed, such countries are actually well placed to take advantage of the coming competition among the Big Three to play off one reserve center against another, bargaining for the best possible terms on new debt issues or for a formal share of international seigniorage revenues.

Neutrality in exchange-regime choice can take the form of a floating rate, the current policy in a sizable number of countries, or it can be implemented as a basket peg, with appropriate weights assigned to each of the Big Three currencies, as well as possibly to others. Floating offers the obvious advantage of adaptability to changing circumstances. Stung by the financial crisis that erupted in 1997, which most analysts attribute at least in part to the dollar-dominated pegs that East Asian governments had tried vainly to defend against unrelenting speculation, many states today are attracted by the alternative of no peg at all—a kind of default strategy that relieves them of any formal obligation to intervene in currency markets. But floating is hardly an all-purpose panacea, as informed observers are now beginning to acknowledge (Cooper, 1999; Hausmann, 1999). In countries where financial markets are still much thinner than in the advanced industrial nations, even small movements into or out of a currency can spell massive exchange-rate volatility. Not all governments may be prepared to live forever with persistent and often arbitrary currency swings. For many, an appropriately weighted basket might not look so bad after all. The pros and cons of basket pegging have long been debated in the formal literature, going back to early contributions by William Branson and Louka Katseli-Papaefstratiou (1980, 1982). As a device to preserve a degree of currency neutrality as well as stability, basket pegging has recently been forcefully advocated as an alternative to floating, especially for the Asia-Pacific region (see, for example, Williamson, 1999).

There is also the option of monetary union—in effect, a strategy of market "alliance" (analogous to a tacit or explicit cartel in an oligopoly).

22

On the model of EMU, local currencies could be merged into one regional money, subordinate to none of the Big Three. Is such an option feasible? Although ardently advocated by some (for example, Walter, 1998), the possibility of monetary union in East Asia or Latin America has been dismissed by others as impractical on economic grounds (for example, Eichengreen and Bayoumi, 1999; Hausmann et al., 1999; Levy Yeyati and Sturzenegger, 2000). Neither East Asians nor Latin Americans, we are told, come even close to approximating an optimum currency area (OCA). In particular, economic shocks tend to be highly asymmetric, threatening to make management of a single monetary policy in either region highly difficult. Until more of the criteria of OCA theory are satisfied, therefore, governments supposedly will hesitate to take the plunge.

Such arguments, however, are deficient in at least three respects. First, much depends on whether divergences among economies are to be regarded as exogenous or endogenous. A celebrated study by Frankel and Rose (1997) shows, for a large sample of countries, a strong positive relation between bilateral trade intensity and the correlation of business cycles, suggesting that monetary union, by promoting higher volumes of trade, might lead to a significant reduction of asymmetric shocks. Separately, Rose (2000) has established that a common currency may increase trade among partner countries by as much as a factor of three.

Second, much also depends on whether the standard conditions identified in OCA theory are, in fact, the most relevant economic variables to consider. Buiter (2000) makes a strong case for the view that conventional OCA theory seriously misleads by assuming that the exchange rate effectively clears the trade balance. In effect, this presupposes a world without financial capital mobility—a world that is obviously at variance with the reality confronting most governments in East Asia and Latin America.

Finally, such arguments again discount the political dimension, which, in the history of monetary unions, has been central. In fact, among all cases of currency unification in the last two centuries, it is impossible to find a single example that was motivated exclusively, or even predominantly, by the concerns highlighted in OCA theory. Political objectives have always predominated. Today, one relevant political objective could well be to avoid dependence on larger outsiders. For this reason alone, the plausibility of the market-alliance option should not be underestimated. Even Mundell (1998), the father of OCA theory, acknowledges that when it comes to a merger of national monetary sovereignties, politics trumps economics.

In short, below the peak of the Currency Pyramid, outcomes will defy easy generalization. Although some states no doubt will be attracted by the security of a followership strategy, sheltering under the wing of one of the Big Three, many others are more likely to prefer to preserve for themselves some room for maneuver in the event of unanticipated circumstances—some more palatable compromise between a government's desire to reduce exchange-rate uncertainty and its legitimate determination to guard against political uncertainty. Many national monies will continue to fight for their own market share, even while others may join together in regional unions or in broader monetary blocs. The geography of money in coming decades will be anything but simple.

4 Technological Developments

Finally, we have to take into consideration one last factor, prospective technological developments, which over the longer term could add even more complexity to tomorrow's monetary landscape. Today's world, I have noted, is still dominated by state currencies. But that will not be so forever. Assuming that current technological trends persist, it is only a matter of time before various innovative forms of money based on digital data—collectively known as "electronic money"—begin to substitute in one way or another for bank notes and checking accounts as customary means of payment. A century from now, electronic money could be in wide circulation, commanding the same general acceptability currently enjoyed by conventional currencies. Once that happens, the geography of money will be even more fundamentally transformed, with currency domains then defined exclusively in the virtual landscapes of cyberspace. Governments will be obliged to compete not only with one another, but also with an increasingly diverse range of private issuers of money. Implications for life at the top of the Currency Pyramid will be truly profound.

From Deterritorialization to Denationalization

The issue may be simply stated. Even with currency deterritorialization, states today still dominate the supply side of the market, retaining jurisdiction over the issue of the monies that most people continue to use. Governments may no longer be able to enforce an exclusive role for their own currency within established political frontiers; that is, they may no longer be able to exercise the monopoly control they once claimed over demand. As the main source of the supply of money, however, they are still in a favored position (like oligopolists) to influence demand insofar as they can successfully compete inside and across borders for the allegiance of market agents. To the extent that user preferences can be swayed, therefore, governments retain some measure of power.

Even that limited measure of power, however, can be retained only so long as states collectively remain dominant on the supply side of the market. Significantly, voices have long been heard opposing even that much government "interference," preferring, instead, to leave money creation solely in the hands of private financial institutions in a world of truly unrestricted currency competition. Envisioned is a system of effectively deterritorialized money shaped exclusively by market forces— *denationalized* money, as the idea was called by its best-known advocate, the late Friedrich von Hayek (1990). Although Hayek's influential laissez-faire views have been echoed by other economists in both Europe and the United States, however, they have thus far failed to enter the mainstream of professional thinking on monetary management. A variety of denationalized currencies already exist, both domestically and internationally, to rival the official issue of central banks, but none has as yet had any but a marginal impact on state dominance of the supply side

At the domestic level, as already observed, diverse private monies circulate in a number of countries. Such currencies, however, are little different from institutionalized systems of multilateral barter, and none trades across national frontiers. At the international level, private substitutes for state monies have long existed in the form of so-called "artificial currency units" (ACUs)—nonstate alternatives designed to perform one or more of the conventional roles of money. Traditionally, though, most ACUs have functioned mainly as a unit of account or store of value, rather than as a medium of exchange, thus posing little direct threat to government dominance of supply. In recent years, the only nonstate form of money that has been used to any substantial degree in international markets is a pool of privately issued assets denominated in European currency units (ECUs), the European Union's old currency unit that came into existence with the European Monetary System in 1979 (now replaced by EMU). Despite having attained limited success in global financial markets, however, the ECU was never widely accepted for private transactional purposes. The IMF's Special Drawing Rights (SDRs) are also a form of artificial currency unit, but for official use only, to be traded among governments or between governments and the IMF.

But now consider electronic money, a technological breakthrough that many specialists think is only a matter of time in coming, given the rapid growth of commerce across the Internet and World Wide Web. Around the globe, entrepreneurs and institutions are racing to develop effective means of payment for the expanding realm of cyberspace. The aim is to create units of purchasing power that are fully usable and transferable electronically: virtual money that can be employed as easily as conventional money to acquire real goods and services. If and when some of these experiments succeed, governments will face a competitive challenge unlike any in living memory—full-bodied ACUs beyond their individual or even collective control—in short, genuinely denationalized monies to rival existing national currencies. When that occurs, dominance of the supply side, not just demand, will be lost. Hayek's vision of a world of unrestricted currency competition will, like it or not, be realized, and the much-anticipated rivalry of the Big Three could turn out to be little more than a sideshow.

Electronic money (also variously labeled "digital currency," "computer money," or "e-cash") comes in two basic forms, smart cards and network money. Both are based on encrypted strings of digits—information coded into series of zeros and ones—that can be transmitted and processed electronically. Smart cards, a technological descendant of the ubiquitous credit card, have an embedded microprocessor (a chip) that is loaded with a monetary value. Versions of the smart card (or "electronic purse") range from simple debit cards, which are typically usable only for a single purpose and may require online authorization for value transfer, to more sophisticated stored-value devices that are reloadable, can be used for multiple purposes, and are off-line capable. Network money stores value in computer hard drives and consists of diverse software products that allow the transfer of purchasing power across electronic networks.

Both forms of electronic money are still in their infancy. Earliest versions, going back a half decade or more, aimed simply to facilitate the settlement of payments electronically. These included diverse card-based systems with names like Mondex and Visa Cash as well as such network-based systems as DigiCash, CyberCash, NetCash, and First Virtual. Operating on the principle of full prepayment by users, each functioned as not much more than a convenient proxy for conventional money—something akin to a glorified travelers check. The velocity of circulation was affected, but money supply was not. None of these systems caught on with the general public, and most have already passed into history ("E-cash 2.0," 2000, p. 67).

More recent versions, mostly network-based, have been more ambitious, aspiring to produce genuine substitutes for conventional money. Most widely advertised in the United States (using Whoopie Goldberg as a spokesperson) is Flooz, a form of gift currency that can be used for purchases from a variety of web sites. Other examples include Beenz, Cybergold, and (in Britain) iPoints. All can be obtained by means other than full prepayment of conventional money, usually as a reward for buying products or services from designated vendors. Like the green stamps or plaid stamps of an earlier era or the frequent-flyer miles of today's airline industry, each can be held more or less indefinitely as a store of value and then eventually employed as a medium of exchange.

Although none of these experimental units has yet been adopted widely, smart cards and network money clearly have the capacity to grow into something far more innovative, given sufficient time and ingenuity. Certainly the incentive is there. Electronic commerce is growing by leaps and bounds, offering both rising transactional volume and a fertile field for experimentation. The stimulus for innovation lies in the promise of seigniorage. Money can be made by making money. This motive alone should ensure that all types of enterprises and institutions—nonbanks as well as banks—will do everything they can to promote new forms of e-currency wherever and whenever they can. As one source puts it: "The companies that control this process will have the opportunity to make money through seigniorage, the traditional profit governments derived from minting money. Electronic seigniorage will be a key to accumulating wealth and power in the twenty-first century" (Weatherford, 1997, pp. 245–246).

Central will be the ability of these companies to find attractive and, more importantly, credible ways to offer smart cards or network money on *credit*, denominated in newly coined digital units like Flooz or Beenz, in the same way that commercial banks have long created money by making loans denominated in state-sanctioned units of account. The opportunity for "virtual" lending lies in the issuers' float: the volume of unclaimed e-money liabilities. Insofar as claimants choose to hold their e-money balances for some time as a store of value, rather than cash them in immediately, resources will become available for generating yet more units of effective purchasing power. Moreover, as general liabilities of their issuers, these new virtual monies could circulate freely from user to user without requiring settlement through the commercial-banking system (that is, without

27

debiting or crediting third-party accounts). "Circling in cyberspace indefinitely," as Elinor Solomon (1997, p. 75) puts it, electronic money would thus substitute fully for existing national currencies. At that point, the infant will have reached maturity.

Maturation will not happen overnight, of course—quite the contrary. The process is apt to be slow and could take most of the next century to be completed. To begin, a number of complex technical issues will have to be addressed, including, *inter alia*, adequate provisions for security (protection against theft or fraud), anonymity (assurance of privacy), and portability (independence of physical location). None of these challenges is apt to be resolved swiftly or painlessly.

Even more critical is the issue of trust: how to command confidence in any new brand of money, given the inertias that generally typify currency use. The conservative bias of the marketplace is a serious obstacle but not an insuperable one. As the volume of electronic commerce grows, it seems almost inevitable that so, too, will brand-name recognition and trust. Another lesson from monetary history is that even if adoption begins slowly, once a critical mass is attained, widespread acceptance will follow. The success of any new brand of currency will depend first and foremost on the inventiveness of its originators in designing features to encourage use. These "bells and whistles" might include favorable rates of exchange when amounts of electronic money are initially acquired, attractive rates of interest on unused balances, assured access to a broad network of other transactors and purveyors, and discounts or bonuses when the electronic money, rather than more traditional currency, is used for purchases or invest-ments. Sooner or later, at least some of these efforts to whet user appetite are bound to achieve success.

Most critical of all is the question of value, how safely to preserve the purchasing power of electronic money balances over time. Initially at least, this is likely to require a promise of full and unrestricted converti-bility into more conventional legal tender—just as early paper monies first gained wide acceptance by a promise of convertibility into precious metal. But just as paper monies eventually took on a life of their own, delinked from a specie base, so, too, might electronic money be able to dispense with all such formal guarantees one day as a result of growing use and familiarity. That day will not come soon, but, given current trends, it seems the most plausible scenario for the more distant future. As *The Economist* ("Electronic Money," 1994, p. 23) once wrote, "[over the long term,] it is possible to imagine the development of e-cash reaching [a] final evolutionary stage . . . in which convertibility into legal tender ceases to be a condition for electronic money; and electronic money will thereby become indistinguishable from—because it will be the same as—other, more traditional sorts of money." When that day finally dawns, perhaps one or two generations from now, we could find a monetary landscape literally teeming with currencies in competition for the allegiance of transactors and investors. In the words of banker Walter Wriston (1998, p. 340): "The Information Standard has replaced the gold-exchange standard. . . . As in ancient times, anyone can announce the issuance of his or her brand of private cash and then try to convince people that it has value. There is no lack of entrants to operate these new private mints ranging from Microsoft to Mondex, and more enter every day."

How Many Currencies?

How many currencies might eventually emerge? Almost certainly, it will not be the "thousands of forms of currency" predicted by anthropologist Jack Weatherford (1998, p. 100), who suggests that "in the future, everyone will be issuing currency—banks, corporations, credit card companies, finance companies, local communities, computer companies, Net browsers, and even individuals. We might have Warren Buffet or William Gates money." Colorful though Weatherford's prediction may be, it neglects the powerful force of network externalities in monetary use, which dictates a preference for fewer, rather than more, monies in circulation. No doubt, there will be much market experimentation, and thousands of forms of e-currency might indeed be tried. But after an inevitable sorting-out process, the number of monies that actually succeed in gaining some degree of general acceptance is sure to be reduced dramatically. Many currencies, unable to compete effectively, will simply disappear.

But neither is it likely that the number of monies will be reduced to as few as one, as Roland Vaubel has contended, exclusively stressing the power of economies of scale. In Vaubel's words (1977): "Ultimately, currency competition destroys itself because the use of money is subject to very sizable economies of scale (p. 437). . . . The only lasting result will be . . . the survival of the fittest currency" (p. 440). In fact, economies of scale are not the only consideration that matters, as modern network theory teaches. Of equal importance are considerations of stability and credibility, which suggest that the optimal number of monies in a world of unrestrained currency competition will actually be significantly greater than one (Thygesen et al., 1995, pp. 39–45).

In network theory, two distinct structures are recognized in the configuration of spatial relations: the "infrastructure," which is the functional basis of a network, and the "infostructure," which provides needed management and control services. Economies of scale, by reducing transactions costs, promote a consolidation of networks at the level of infrastructure, just as Vaubel argues. At the infostructure level, by contrast, the optimal configuration tends to be rather more decentralized and competitive, in order to maximize agent responsibility. Some finite number of rival networks will counter the negative effects of absolute monopoly, which frequently leads to weakened control by users and diluted incentives for suppliers. Thus, a rational tradeoff exists for market agents, an impulse for some degree of diversification that will most likely result in an equilibrium outcome short of complete centralization. In the monetary geography of the future, a smallish population of currencies is far more probable than a single universal money.

Implications for the Big Three

Where will all this leave today's Big Three? Until now, the top international currencies have enjoyed something of a free ride—all the benefits of competitive success abroad without the corresponding disadvantages of a threat to monetary monopoly at home. In these economies, there has not yet been any real erosion of monetary powers. For them, therefore, the advent of electronic money will represent an unprecedented challenge. Once e-monies begin to gain widespread acceptance, the market leaders, too, like countries further down the Currency Pyramid, will face genuine currency competition on their own turf.

Indeed, the challenge of electronic money is likely to be felt by the market leaders first, even before its impact spreads to countries with less competitive currencies. The reason is evident. It is the Big Three that are most "wired," the most plugged in to the new realm of electronic commerce. Thus, if electronic money is to gain widespread acceptance anywhere, it will most probably happen initially in the United States, Europe, and Japan. It is no accident that Flooz, Beenz, and most other early experiments have originated in the world's most advanced economies, which are both financially sophisticated and computer literate. It is precisely these economies that are likely to be the most receptive to innovative new means of payment that can be used and transferred electronically.

Domestically, the effect will be a significant erosion in the effectiveness of monetary policy. Each of the Big Three central banks—the

Federal Reserve, the ECB, and the Bank of Japan— may still be able to exercise a degree of control over monetary aggregates denominated in the economy's own currency unit. But with new electronic monies also in use, variations in the supply of commercial-bank reserves will have correspondingly less influence on the overall level of spending. As other countries with less competitive monies have already discovered, substitute currencies mean alternative circuits of spending, affecting prices and employment, and alternative settlement systems that are not directly affected by the traditional instruments of policy. As Benjamin Friedman (1999, p. 335) puts the point, "currency substitution opens the way for what amounts to competition among national clearing mechanisms, even if each is maintained by a different country's central bank in its own currency." Electronic money, Friedman (1999, p. 321) continues, will have the same effect. Monetary policy could become little more than a device to signal the authorities' preferences. The central bank would become not much more than "an army with only a signal corps."

Externally, the effect could be a substantial reshuffling of standing in the Currency Pyramid. Even a small population of currencies will continue to display characteristics of hierarchy, reflecting varying degrees of competitive strength. The currencies that disappear, including many of the newer e-monies as well as older national currencies, will be those that cannot survive the Darwinian process of natural selection. There is no reason to believe that the dollar, euro, and yen will be unable to compete effectively even far into the next century.

There is also no reason to believe, however, that in that more distant future, the Big Three will continue to monopolize the peak of the Currency Pyramid. There may be no serious challengers to their dominance among currencies in circulation today, which are all state currencies, but there could well be serious challengers among the electronic monies of tomorrow, which will be largely private. Microsoft money could, in time, become more popular than dollars. As the deputy governor of the Bank of England (*New York Times*, December 20, 1999, p. C3) has suggested, "the successors to Bill Gates [could] put the successors to Alan Greenspan out of business." Otmar Issing of the ECB puts the point even more harshly. In a world of electronic money, Issing (1999, p. 21) asks, "would the familiar existing units of account, the euro, the US dollar, the pound sterling, etc., continue to mean anything?" By the end of the twenty-first century, life at the top might look very different indeed.

31

5 Conclusion

The conclusions of this essay can be summarized briefly. Prospects for the top international currencies differ considerably, depending on the time horizon in question. In the near term, the position of the Big Three at the peak of the Currency Pyramid looks secure, with no immediate challenger in sight. Relative standings could shift substantially, however, with the euro gaining on the dollar in market competition and the yen possibly fading to an even more distant third place. As a result, policy rivalry among the market leaders will almost certainly intensify, in turn compelling governments elsewhere to reconsider their own strategic preferences. Some countries will undoubtedly opt to tie their currencies closely to one of the Big Three, promoting the coalescence of two or possibly three large monetary blocs. Many others will choose to remain more neutral, however, and some may be tempted by the precedent of EMU to try merging their currencies into regional monetary unions in order to sustain or promote user loyalty.

Beyond the near term, by contrast, the position of the Big Three looks less secure, not because any existing national currency will pose a challenge, but because future private monies are likely to develop in the virtual world of cyberspace. The twenty-first century will introduce the era of electronic monies—monies that are not only deterritorialized but denationalized as well. Some of these new monies may eventually hold more market appeal than any of today's top international currencies.

References

Aliber, Robert Z., *The International Money Game*, 5th ed., New York, Basic Books, 1987.

"Asian Currencies: Swapping Notes," *The Economist*, May 13, 2000, pp. 76–77.

Bank for International Settlements, *Central Bank Survey of Foreign Exchange and Derivatives Market Activity 1998*, Basle, Bank for International Settlements, 1999.

Beddoes, Zanny Minton, "From EMU to AMU? The Case for Regional Currencies," *Foreign Affairs*, 78 (July/August 1999), pp. 8–13.

Bénassy-Quéré, Agnès, and Amina Lahrèche-Révil, "The Euro and Southern Mediterranean Countries," Paris, Centre d'Études Prospectives et d'Informations Internationales, 1999, processed.

Bergsten, C. Fred, "The Impact of the Euro on Exchange Rates and International Policy Cooperation," in Paul R. Masson, Thomas H. Krueger, and Bart G. Turtelboom, eds., *EMU and the International Monetary System*, Washington, D.C., International Monetary Fund, 1997, chap. 2.

———, "Missed Opportunity," *The International Economy*, 12 (November/December 1998), pp. 26–27.

Blinder, Alan S., "The Role of the Dollar as an International Currency," *Eastern Economic Journal*, 22 (Spring 1996), pp. 127–136.

Branson, William H., and Louka T. Katseli-Papaefstratiou, "Income Instability, Terms of Trade, and the Choice of an Exchange Rate Regime," *Journal of Development Economics*, 7 (March 1980), pp. 49–69.

———, "Currency Baskets and Real Effective Exchange Rates," in Mark Gersovitz, ed., *The Theory and Experience of Economic Development: Essays in Honor of Sir Arthur Lewis*, London, Allen and Unwin, 1982, pp. 194–214.

Buiter, Willem H., "Optimal Currency Areas: Why Does the Exchange Rate Regime Matter?" CEPR Discussion Paper No. 2366, London, Centre for Economic Policy Research, January 2000.

Cohen, Benjamin J., *The Future of Sterling as an International Currency*, London, Macmillan, 1971.

———, *In Whose Interest? International Banking and American Foreign Policy*, New Haven, Conn., Yale University Press, 1986.

———, *The Geography of Money*, Ithaca, N.Y., Cornell University Press, 1998.

———, "Beyond EMU: The Problem of Sustainability," in Barry Eichengreen and Jeffry Frieden, eds., *The Political Economy of European Monetary Unification*, 2nd ed., Boulder, Colo., Westview, 2000.

———, "Dollarisation: Le Dimension Politique," *L'Économie Politique*, 5 (January 2000), pp. 88–112.

Cooper, Richard N., "Should Capital Controls Be Banished?" *Brookings Papers on Economic Activity*, No. 1, (1999), pp. 89–125.

Council of Economic Advisers, *Annual Report*, Washington, D.C., Government Printing Office, 1999.

Danthine, Jean-Pierre, Francesco Giavazzi, and Ernst-Ludwig von Thadden, "European Financial Markets After EMU: A First Assessment," CEPR Discussion Paper No. 2413, London, Centre for Economic Policy Research, April 2000.

De Boissieu, Christian, "Concurrence entre Monnaies et Polycentrisme Monétaire," in Donald E. Fair and Christian De Boissieu, eds., *International Monetary and Financial Integration—The European Dimension*, Boston, Kluwer, 1988, chap. 13.

Detken, Carsten, and Philipp Hartmann, "The Euro and International Capital Markets," *International Finance*, 3 (April 2000), pp. 53–94.

Deutsche Bundesbank, "The Circulation of Deutsche Marks Abroad," *Monthly Report of the Deutsche Bundesbank*, 47 (July 1995), pp. 65–71.

Dornbusch, Rudiger, "The Euro: Implications for Latin America," Washington, D.C., World Bank, 1999, processed.

Dowd, Kevin, and David Greenaway, "Currency Competition, Network Externalities and Switching Costs: Towards an Alternative View of Optimum Currency Areas," *Economic Journal*, 103 (September 1993), pp. 1180–1189.

"E-cash 2.0," *The Economist*, February 19, 2000, pp. 67–71.

Eichengreen, Barry, *International Monetary Arrangements for the 21st Century*, Washington, D.C., Brookings Institution, 1994.

Eichengreen, Barry, and Tamim Bayoumi, "Is Asia an Optimum Currency Area? Can It Become One? Regional, Global, and Historical Perspectives on Asian Monetary Relations," in Stefan Collignon, Jean Pisani-Ferry, and Yung Chul Park, eds., *Exchange Rate Policies in Emerging Asian Countries*, London, Routledge, 1999, chap. 21.

"Electronic Money: So Much for the Cashless Society," *The Economist*, November 26, 1994, pp. 21–23.

European Central Bank (ECB) "International Role of the Euro," *Monthly Bulletin* (August 1999), pp. 31–53.

Frankel, Jeffrey A., *No Single Currency Regime is Right for All Countries or at All Times*, Essays in International Finance No. 215, Princeton, N.J. Princeton University, International Finance Section, August 1999.

Frankel, Jeffrey A., and Andrew K. Rose, "The Endogeneity of the Optimum Currency Area Criteria," *Economic Journal*, 108 (July 1997), pp. 1009–1025.

Friedman, Benjamin M., "The Future of Monetary Policy: The Central Bank as an Army with Only a Signal Corps?" *International Finance*, 2 (November 1999), pp. 321–338.

Goodhart, Charles A. E., "The Political Economy of Monetary Union," in Peter B. Kenen, ed., *Understanding Interdependence: The Macroeconomics of the Open Economy*, Princeton, N.J., Princeton University Press, 1995, chap. 12.

Hale, David D., "Is it a Yen or a Dollar Crisis in the Currency Market?" *Washington Quarterly*, 18 (Autumn 1995), pp. 145–171.

Hartmann, Philipp, *Currency Competition and Foreign Exchange Markets: The Dollar, the Yen and the Euro*, Cambridge and New York, Cambridge University Press, 1998.

Hausmann, Ricardo, "Should There Be Five Currencies or One Hundred and Five?" *Foreign Policy*, 116 (Fall 1999), pp. 65–79.

Hausmann, Ricardo, Michael Gavin, Carmen Pages-Serra, and Ernesto Stein, "Financial Turmoil and the Choice of Exchange Rate Regime," Working Paper No. 400, Washington, D.C., Inter-American Development Bank, 1999.

Hayek, Friedrich von, *Denationalisation of Money—The Argument Refined*, 3rd ed., London, Institute of Economic Affairs, 1990.

Honohan, Patrick, and Philip Lane, "Will the Euro Trigger More Monetary Unions in Africa?" paper prepared for a World Institute for Development Economics Research (WIDER) Conference on EMU and Its Impact on Europe and the Developing Countries, Helsinki, Finland, November 11–12, 1999.

Hoshi, Takeo, and Anil Kashyap, "The Japanese Banking Crisis: Where Did It Come from and Where Will It End?" *NBER Macroeconomics Annual 1999*, Cambridge, Mass., MIT Press, 2000, pp. 129–201.

Hughes, Christopher W., "Japanese Policy and the East Asian Currency Crisis: Abject Defeat or Quiet Victory?" *Review of International Political Economy*, 7 (Summer 2000), pp. 219–253.

International Monetary Fund (IMF), *Results of the 1997 Coordinated Portfolio Investment Survey*, Washington, D.C., International Monetary Fund, 1999.

Issing, Otmar, "Hayek—Currency Competition and European Monetary Union," Annual Hayek Memorial Lecture, London, Institute of Economic Affairs, May 27, 1999, processed.

Ito, Takatoshi, and Michael Melvin, "The Political Economy of Japan's Big Bang," in Magnus Blomstrom, Byron Gangnes, and Sumner La Croix, eds., *Japan's New Economy: Continuity and Change in the Twenty-First Century*, New York, Oxford University Press, 2000, pp. 162–174.

Joint Economic Committee of the U.S. Congress, *Joint Economic Report 1999*, Washington, D.C., Government Printing Office, 1999.

Krueger, Russell, and Jiming Ha, "Measurement of Cocirculation of Currencies," in Paul D. Mizen and Eric J. Pentecost, eds., *The Macroeconomics of International Currencies: Theory, Policy and Evidence*, Brookfield, Vt., Elgar, 1996, chap. 4.

Krugman, Paul R., "The International Role of the Dollar," in Krugman, *Currencies and Crises*, Cambridge, Mass., MIT Press, 1992, chap. 10.

Levy Yeyati, Eduardo, and Federico Sturzenegger, "Is EMU a Blueprint for Mercosur?" *Latin American Journal of Economics*, 110 (April 2000), pp. 63–99.

Makinen, Gail E., "Euro Currency: How Much Could It Cost the United States?" CRS Report 98–998E, Washington, D.C., Congressional Research Service, 1998.

Mundell, Robert A., "European Monetary Union and the International Monetary System," in Ario Baldassarri, Cesare Imbriani, Dominick Salvatore, eds., *The International System between New Integration and Neo-Protectionism*, Central Issues in Contemporary Economic Theory and Policy Series, New York, St. Martin's, and London, Macmillan, 1996, pp. 81–128.

————, "The Case for the Euro," *Wall Street Journal*, March 24, 1998, p. A22.

Orléan, André, "Mimetic Contagion and Speculative Bubbles," *Theory and Decision*, 27 (No. 1–2, 1989), pp. 63–92.

Porter, Richard D., and Ruth A. Judson, "The Location of U.S. Currency: How Much Is Abroad? *Federal Reserve Bulletin*, 82 (October 1996), pp. 883–903.

Portes, Richard, "Global Financial Markets and Financial Stability: Europe's Role," CEPR Discussion Paper No. 2298, London, Centre for Economic Policy Research, November 1999.

Portes, Richard, and Hélène Rey, "The Emergence of the Euro as an International Currency," in David Begg, Jürgen von Hagen, Charles Wyplosz, and Klaus F. Zimmermann, eds., *EMU: Prospects and Challenges for the Euro*, Oxford, Blackwell, 1998, pp. 307–343.

Rogoff, Kenneth, "Blessing or Curse? Foreign and Underground Demand for Euro Notes," in David Begg, Jürgen von Hagen, Charles Wyplosz, and Klaus

F. Zimmerman, eds., *EMU: Prospects and Challenges for the Euro*, Oxford, Blackwell, 1998, pp. 261–303.

Rose, Andrew K., "One Money, One Market: The Effect of Common Currencies on Trade," *Economic Policy*, 30 (April 2000), pp. 7–45.

Schaede, Ulrike, "After the Bubble: Evaluating Financial Reform in Japan in the 1990s," San Diego, Calif., University of California at San Diego, 2000, processed.

Solomon, Elinor Harris, *Virtual Money: Understanding the Power and Risks of Money's High-Speed Journey into Electronic Space*, New York, Oxford University Press, 1997.

Solomon, Lewis D., *Rethinking Our Centralized Monetary System: The Case for a System of Local Currencies*, Westport, Conn., Praeger, 1996.

Thygesen, Niels, and the ECU Institute, *International Currency Competition and the Future Role of the Single European Currency*, Final Report of the Working Group on "European Monetary Union—International Monetary System," London and Boston, Kluwer Law International, 1995.

Vaubel, Roland, "Free Currency Competition," *Weltwirtschafliches Archiv*, 113 (No. 3, 1977), pp. 435–461.

Walter, Norbert, "An Asian Prediction," *The International Economy*, 12 (May/June 1998), p. 49.

Weatherford, Jack, *The History of Money*, New York, Three Rivers Press, 1997.

———, "Cash in a Cul-de-Sac," in "The Fiscal Frontier," *Discover*, 19 (October 1998), p. 100.

Williamson, John, "The Case for a Common Basket Peg for East Asian Currencies," in Stefan Collignon, Jean Pisani-Ferry, and Yung Chul Park, eds., *Exchange Rate Policies in Emerging Asian Countries*, London, Routledge, 1999, chap. 19.

Wriston, Walter B., "Dumb Networks and Smart Capital," *Cato Journal*, 17 (Winter 1998), pp. 333–344.

Wyplosz, Charles, "An International Role for the Euro?" in Jean Dermine and Pierre Hillion, eds., *European Capital Markets with a Single Currency*, Oxford, Oxford University Press, 1999, chap. 3.

PUBLICATIONS OF THE
INTERNATIONAL ECONOMICS SECTION

Notice to Contributors

The International Economics Section publishes papers in two series. ESSAYS IN INTERNATIONAL ECONOMICS and PRINCETON STUDIES IN INTERNATIONAL ECONOMICS. Two earlier series, REPRINTS IN INTERNATIONAL FINANCE and SPECIAL PAPERS IN INTERNATIONAL ECONOMICS, have been discontinued, with the SPECIAL PAPERS being absorbed into the STUDIES series.

The Section welcomes the submission of manuscripts focused on topics in international trade, international macroeconomics, or international finance. Submissions should address systemic issues for the global economy or, if concentrating on particular economies, should adopt a comparative perspective.

ESSAYS IN INTERNATIONAL ECONOMICS are meant to disseminate new views about international economic events and policy issues. They should be accessible to a broad audience of professional economists.

PRINCETON STUDIES IN INTERNATIONAL ECONOMICS are devoted to new research in international economics or to synthetic treatments of a body of literature. They should be comparable in originality and technical proficiency to papers published in leading economic journals. Papers that are longer and more complete than those publishable in the professional journals are welcome.

Manuscripts should be submitted in triplicate, typed single sided and double spaced throughout on 8½ by 11 white bond paper. Publication can be expedited if manuscripts are computer keyboarded in WordPerfect or a compatible program. Additional instructions and a style guide are available from the Section or on the website at www.princeton.edu/~ies.

How to Obtain Publications

The Section's publications are distributed free of charge to college, university, and public libraries and to nongovernmental, nonprofit research institutions. Eligible institutions may ask to be placed on the Section's permanent mailing list.

Individuals and institutions not qualifying for free distribution may receive all publications for the calendar year for a subscription fee of $45.00. Late subscribers will receive all back issues for the year during which they subscribe.

Publications may be ordered individually, with payment made in advance. ESSAYS and REPRINTS cost $10.00 each; STUDIES and SPECIAL PAPERS cost $13.50. An additional $1.50 should be sent for postage and handling within the United States, Canada, and Mexico; $2.25 should be added for surface delivery outside the region.

All payments must be made in U.S. dollars. Subscription fees and charges for single issues will be waived for organizations and individuals in countries where foreign-exchange regulations prohibit dollar payments.

Information about the Section and its publishing program is available on the Section's website at www.princeton.edu/~ies. A subscription and order form is printed at the end of this volume. Correspondence should be addressed to:

International Economics Section
Department of Economics, Fisher Hall
Princeton University
Princeton, New Jersey 08544-1021
Tel: 609-258-4048 • Fax: 609-258-1374
E-mail: ies@princeton.edu

List of Recent Publications

A complete list of publications is available at the International Economics Section website at www.princeton.edu/~ies.

ESSAYS IN INTERNATIONAL ECONOMICS
(formerly Essays in International Finance)

182. Tommaso Padoa-Schioppa, ed., with Michael Emerson, Kumiharu Shigehara, and Richard Portes, *Europe After 1992: Three Essays*. (May 1991)
183. Michael Bruno, *High Inflation and the Nominal Anchors of an Open Economy*. (June 1991)
184. Jacques J. Polak, *The Changing Nature of IMF Conditionality*. (September 1991)
185. Ethan B. Kapstein, *Supervising International Banks: Origins and Implications of the Basle Accord*. (December 1991)
186. Alessandro Giustiniani, Francesco Papadia, and Daniela Porciani, *Growth and Catch-Up in Central and Eastern Europe: Macroeconomic Effects on Western Countries*. (April 1992)
187. Michele Fratianni, Jürgen von Hagen, and Christopher Waller, *The Maastricht Way to EMU*. (June 1992)
188. Pierre-Richard Agénor, *Parallel Currency Markets in Developing Countries: Theory, Evidence, and Policy Implications*. (November 1992)
189. Beatriz Armendariz de Aghion and John Williamson, *The G-7's Joint-and-Several Blunder*. (April 1993)
190. Paul Krugman, *What Do We Need to Know about the International Monetary System?* (July 1993)
191. Peter M. Garber and Michael G. Spencer, *The Dissolution of the Austro-Hungarian Empire: Lessons for Currency Reform*. (February 1994)
192. Raymond F. Mikesell, *The Bretton Woods Debates: A Memoir*. (March 1994)
193. Graham Bird, *Economic Assistance to Low-Income Countries: Should the Link be Resurrected?* (July 1994)
194. Lorenzo Bini-Smaghi, Tommaso Padoa-Schioppa, and Francesco Papadia, *The Transition to EMU in the Maastricht Treaty*. (November 1994)
195. Ariel Buira, *Reflections on the International Monetary System*. (January 1995)
196. Shinji Takagi, *From Recipient to Donor: Japan's Official Aid Flows, 1945 to 1990 and Beyond*. (March 1995)
197. Patrick Conway, *Currency Proliferation: The Monetary Legacy of the Soviet Union*. (June 1995)
198. Barry Eichengreen, *A More Perfect Union? The Logic of Economic Integration*. (June 1996)
199. Peter B. Kenen, ed., with John Arrowsmith, Paul De Grauwe, Charles A. E. Goodhart, Daniel Gros, Luigi Spaventa, and Niels Thygesen, *Making EMU Happen—Problems and Proposals: A Symposium*. (August 1996)
200. Peter B. Kenen, ed., with Lawrence H. Summers, William R. Cline, Barry Eichengreen, Richard Portes, Arminio Fraga, and Morris Goldstein, *From Halifax to Lyons: What Has Been Done about Crisis Management?* (October 1996)

201. Louis W. Pauly, *The League of Nations and the Foreshadowing of the International Monetary Fund*. (December 1996)
202. Harold James, *Monetary and Fiscal Unification in Nineteenth-Century Germany: What Can Kohl Learn from Bismarck?* (March 1997)
203. Andrew Crockett, *The Theory and Practice of Financial Stability*. (April 1997)
204. Benjamin J. Cohen, *The Financial Support Fund of the OECD: A Failed Initiative*. (June 1997)
205. Robert N. McCauley, *The Euro and the Dollar*. (November 1997)
206. Thomas Laubach and Adam S. Posen, *Disciplined Discretion: Monetary Targeting in Germany and Switzerland*. (December 1997)
207. Stanley Fischer, Richard N. Cooper, Rudiger Dornbusch, Peter M. Garber, Carlos Massad, Jacques J. Polak, Dani Rodrik, and Savak S. Tarapore, *Should the IMF Pursue Capital-Account Convertibility?* (May 1998)
208. Charles P. Kindleberger, *Economic and Financial Crises and Transformations in Sixteenth-Century Europe*. (June 1998)
209. Maurice Obstfeld, *EMU: Ready or Not?* (July 1998)
210. Wilfred Ethier, *The International Commercial System*. (September 1998)
211. John Williamson and Molly Mahar, *A Survey of Financial Liberalization*. (November 1998)
212. Ariel Buira, *An Alternative Approach to Financial Crises*. (February 1999)
213. Barry Eichengreen, Paul Masson, Miguel Savastano, and Sunil Sharma, *Transition Strategies and Nominal Anchors on the Road to Greater Exchange-Rate Flexibility*. (April 1999)
214. Curzio Giannini, *"Enemy of None but a Common Friend of All"? An International Perspective on the Lender-of-Last-Resort Function*. (June 1999)
215. Jeffrey A. Frankel, *No Single Currency Regime Is Right for All Countries or at All Times*. (August 1999)
216. Jacques J. Polak, *Streamlining the Financial Structure of the International Monetary Fund*. (September 1999)
217. Gustavo H. B. Franco, *The Real Plan and the Exchange Rate*. (April 2000)
218. Thomas D. Willett, *International Financial Markets as Sources of Crises or Discipline: The Too Much, Too Late Hypothesis*. (May 2000)
219. Richard H. Clarida, *G-3 Exchange-Rate Relationships: A Review of the Record and of Proposals for Change*. (September 2000)
220. Stanley Fischer, *On the Need for an International Lender of Last Resort*. (November 2000)
221. Benjamin J. Cohen, *Life at the Top: International Currencies in the Twenty-First Century*. (December 2000)

PRINCETON STUDIES IN INTERNATIONAL ECONOMICS
(formerly Princeton Studies in International Finance)

69. Felipe Larraín and Andrés Velasco, *Can Swaps Solve the Debt Crisis? Lessons from the Chilean Experience*. (November 1990)
70. Kaushik Basu, *The International Debt Problem, Credit Rationing and Loan Pushing: Theory and Experience*. (October 1991)

71. Daniel Gros and Alfred Steinherr, *Economic Reform in the Soviet Union: Pas de Deux between Disintegration and Macroeconomic Destabilization.* (November 1991)
72. George M. von Furstenberg and Joseph P. Daniels, *Economic Summit Declarations, 1975-1989: Examining the Written Record of International Cooperation.* (February 1992)
73. Ishac Diwan and Dani Rodrik, *External Debt, Adjustment, and Burden Sharing: A Unified Framework.* (November 1992)
74. Barry Eichengreen, *Should the Maastricht Treaty Be Saved?* (December 1992)
75. Adam Klug, *The German Buybacks, 1932-1939: A Cure for Overhang?* (November 1993)
76. Tamim Bayoumi and Barry Eichengreen, *One Money or Many? Analyzing the Prospects for Monetary Unification in Various Parts of the World.* (September 1994)
77. Edward E. Leamer, *The Heckscher-Ohlin Model in Theory and Practice.* (February 1995)
78. Thorvaldur Gylfason, *The Macroeconomics of European Agriculture.* (May 1995)
79. Angus S. Deaton and Ronald I. Miller, *International Commodity Prices, Macroeconomic Performance, and Politics in Sub-Saharan Africa.* (December 1995)
80. Chander Kant, *Foreign Direct Investment and Capital Flight.* (April 1996)
81. Gian Maria Milesi-Ferretti and Assaf Razin, *Current-Account Sustainability.* (October 1996)
82. Pierre-Richard Agénor, *Capital-Market Imperfections and the Macroeconomic Dynamics of Small Indebted Economies.* (June 1997)
83. Michael Bowe and James W. Dean, *Has the Market Solved the Sovereign-Debt Crisis?* (August 1997)
84. Willem H. Buiter, Giancarlo M. Corsetti, and Paolo A. Pesenti, *Interpreting the ERM Crisis: Country-Specific and Systemic Issues.* (March 1998)
85. Holger C. Wolf, *Transition Strategies: Choices and Outcomes.* (June 1999)
86. Alessandro Prati and Garry J. Schinasi, *Financial Stability in European Economic and Monetary Union.* (August 1999)
87. Peter Hooper, Karen Johnson, and Jaime Marquez, *Trade Elasticities for the G-7 Countries.* (August 2000)

SPECIAL PAPERS IN INTERNATIONAL ECONOMICS

16. Elhanan Helpman, *Monopolistic Competition in Trade Theory.* (June 1990)
17. Richard Pomfret, *International Trade Policy with Imperfect Competition.* (August 1992)
18. Hali J. Edison, *The Effectiveness of Central-Bank Intervention: A Survey of the Literature After 1982.* (July 1993)
19. Sylvester W.C. Eijffinger and Jakob De Haan, *The Political Economy of Central-Bank Independence.* (May 1996)
20. Olivier Jeanne, *Currency Crises: A Perspective on Recent Theoretical Developments.* (March 2000)

REPRINTS IN INTERNATIONAL FINANCE

29. Peter B. Kenen, *Sorting Out Some EMU Issues*; reprinted from Jean Monnet Chair Paper 38, Robert Schuman Centre, European University Institute, 1996. (December 1996)

∘ SUBSCRIBE ∘ ORDER ∘

INTERNATIONAL ECONOMICS SECTION

SUBSCRIPTIONS

Rate	$45 a year

The International Economics Section issues six to eight publications each year in a mix of Essays, Studies, and occasional Reprints. Late subscribers receive all publications for the subscription year. Prepayment is required and may be made by check in U.S. dollars or by Visa or MasterCard. A complete list of publications is available at www.princeton.edu/~ies.

Address inquiries to:

International Economics Section
Department of Economics, Fisher Hall
Princeton University
Princeton, NJ 08544–1021

BOOK ORDERS

Essays & Reprints	$10.00
Studies & Special Papers	$13.50
plus postage	
Within U.S.	$1.50
Outside U.S. (surface mail)	$2.25

_____

Discounts are available for book dealers and for orders of five or more publications.

_____

Telephone: 609–258–4048
Telefax: 609–258–1374
E-mail: ies@princeton.edu

fold up

INTERNATIONAL ECONOMICS SECTION

This is a subscription ☐ ; a book order ☐

Essay #(s) _____, _____ No. of copies___

Study #(s) _____, _____ No. of copies___

Special Paper # _____ No. of copies___

Reprint # _____ No. of copies___

☐ Enclosed is my check made payable to Princeton University, International Economics Section

totaling $_____.

Please charge: ☐ Visa ☐ MasterCard

Acct.# _____

Expires _____

Signature_____

Send to:

Name_____

Address_____

City _____

State _____Zip _____

Country_____

INTERNATIONAL ECONOMICS SECTION
DEPARTMENT OF ECONOMICS
FISHER HALL
PRINCETON UNIVERSITY
PRINCETON, NJ 08544-1021